Table Mentoring

A SIMPLE GUIDE TO COMING ALONGSIDE

SUE MOORE DONALDSON

Dedication

Dedicated to all the women who came alongside ~
devoted first to God,
and then for some wonderful reason,
devoted to me.

#grateful
#everytabletellsastory

Acknowledgements

Thanks goes to special friends who know the value of mentoring and being mentored, and continue to mentor me by example and love: *Carly, Jaime, Brittany, Melody C., Melody H., Laurie, Janelle, Suzanne, Ceslie, Angela, Mabel, Gretchen and Emily.*

I couldn't have done this half so well without my friends, Christiane Flores of Red Letter Arts and Deborah Jeffrey of CupcakeStylist.com.

I appreciate you all for coming alongside.

Contents

Introduction

You may think you need to be older to be a mentor. At least, wiser, smarter, more godly--with more Bible knowledge than a 4th grader in AWANA (or perhaps, a Sparky.) Don't get me wrong. Bible knowledge is a good thing. We can always know more, and I, for one, can always obey better and deeper what I already know.

Table Mentoring: A Simple Guide to Coming Alongside will help you get started sharing your life with someone. Someone who needs to know what you have learned at the feet of Jesus - so that they learn what you've learned. So that they grow up in Jesus. That's the goal. Not only for fun—though it often is; not only to make a new friend—which usually happens. Mentoring, at a table or not, needs to be part of every believer's life. We know God so that we can help another to know God. We come alongside and show the way. And what a gift that is—to the mentor and to the mentee. Blessed to be a blessing.

Wisdom and knowledge and godliness are great attributes, but you may be thinking: how smart or wise or godly do I need to be before I pass on what I know to someone who needs to know it? Is there a measuring stick we place by the door, and when we reach the gold bar of holy living and mature faith, we open the door to becoming a mentor to a younger believer? I don't think so.

There is no right age. There is no way to measure. So, I offer you this: you are old enough (now) to mentor. And you are young enough (now) to be mentored. I know this–I am old— older than many of my relatives. Old enough to know that there is always someone younger than I am who needs to know what I can tell them. And there is always someone older than I am who can pour truth and wisdom into my life.

I offer this simple guidebook to mentoring so you can begin to mentor and be mentored with confidence. You will learn that it doesn't take a seminary degree to begin to obey what God has asked us to do in His name and by His strength. As with all of His commandments, they are for our good and for His glory.

You may not feel adequate to mentor, but if you sense a tug on your heart to come alongside a younger believer, get ready for one of the most exciting adventures of being a Christ-follower.

Not feeling adequate shows that you are more ready than you think.

It's not a matter of resources – you can always find someone to help you help another, if you get stuck. It is a matter of surrender, willingness, courage, dependence, and anticipation of God's power and desire to use you. There is nothing more rewarding than seeing the life of Christ duplicated in the life of another. And to think that He wants to use us to get that accomplished! Amazing!

Paul knew how that felt as he wrote to believers in Thessalonica:

Dear brothers and sisters, we can't help but thank God for you, because your faith is flourishing and your love for one another is growing.
II Thessalonians 1:3 NLT

Paul also knew that feeling inadequate was the secret of his strength:

But he said to me, "My grace is sufficient for you, for my power is made perfect in weakness." Therefore I will boast all the more gladly about my weaknesses, so that Christ's power may rest on me.

II Corinthians 12:9 NIV

Our weakness is the least of God's concerns. He's got that figured out. He does expect us to grow up in Him, and as He leads and matures us, we need to pass on what we learn to someone else. We glorify Him most when we offer ourselves back to Him and allow Him to make us, in the words of Oswald Chambers, "broken bread and poured out wine" for others. And I am always convicted and encouraged when I read the following:

"Whenever you get a blessing from God, give it back to Him as a love gift. Take time to meditate before God and offer the blessing back to Him in a deliberate act of worship. If you hoard a thing for yourself, it will turn into spiritual dry rot, as the manna did when it was hoarded. God will never let you hold a spiritual thing for yourself, it has to be given back to Him that He may make it a blessing to others."

--Oswald Chambers, <u>My Utmost for His Highest</u> (January 6)

We are blessed to be a blessing, not to be dry rot. At any age, at any stage.

1
Table Mentoring:
What Is It?

In my early 20's I met Jeanne Garison. Jeanne was wise, gracious, funny, and for some reason, loved me. She showed it by pouring her wisdom into me, her time into my time, her life into my life. Living life with Jeanne alongside made all the difference.

I was a new college grad—starting my beginning whirl into the real world—single and facing my first career, a new roommate, a new town and a new church family. Not floundering exactly, but needing emotional, practical and spiritual support.

I don't remember how we first met one-on-one. I do remember sitting at Jeanne's table, talking and talking, usually a cup of tea in one hand and a pen in the other. (It was good to have a pen when I spent time with Jeanne.) I also remember Jeanne's response: spoken with a smile, a gentle word, often a chuckle of understanding--never a judgment:

"You know, Sue, this is how it was with my mother."
"Sounds like you could use help in this area – let me get this organized for you."
"The most important thing you can tell your students is that God is your most important thing."

You see why I was grateful. Everyone needs a Jeanne.

In my late 20's I met Karen and Carol, Debbie and Gerri. They were high school Juniors—smart, motivated, filled with dreams and goals, and for some reason, they loved me, too. I asked them one afternoon:

"Would you like to meet with me after school some day--say, Wednesday? We can talk about your dreams and goals, your guy-relationships, your mom-relationships, and most of all, your relationship with God?"

They said, "Yes" and off we went. We met three months, once a week, and then, I sent each on their way: to meet with a Freshman girl—Fresh from our three months, on to a new three months. Table mentoring, one-to-one, one-to-three. Passing on what they knew, what I knew and now, I pass it on to you.

Table mentoring worked. For me, for Jeanne, for high school girls ready to fly. And it can for you, as well.

Table Mentoring: What Is It?

"To mentor" means to advise and counsel another, usually a *younger* another. That makes sense. It's the exception that someone younger knows more than you do in your area of expertise, no matter how young you are. And let's hope that the older we grow, the more we know. But that's another book. The word MENTOR comes from Greek mythology when

Odysseus's trusted counselor, Mentor, was left in charge of his household--specifically to come alongside the younger Telemachus. Mentor is described as "wise and trusted advisor or guide." (*thefreedictionary.com)

In the 70's we used the word DISCIPLE rather than MENTOR, but in the Christian context, it's the same. At that time, I benefitted by reading Anne Ortlund's bestseller *Disciplines of a Beautiful Woman.* It's still in print and I highly recommend it.

Do you need a table to Table Mentor? No. But a table imbues intimacy—an elbow-touching-grab-a-hand-in-prayer type of closeness. Maybe not at the first meet-up, but definitely in the mix along the way.

Table, bench, back steps, dorm hallway, coffee house—choose whichever promotes the progress of a hearty sharing. The place or porch doesn't matter. Taking the time to listen does. Tell a story, gently nudge, cry some, laugh a lot, and give all to the Mighty Counselor before and after and maybe in the middle. Coming together until the misery is out of the commiserate, as you both sit at Jesus' feet.

I love to describe MENTORING as "to come alongside" which is found in *The Message* version of II Corinthians 1: 3 and 4--

"God comes alongside us when we go through hard times, and before you know it, He brings us alongside someone else who is going through hard times so that we can be there for that person just as God was there for us."
II Corinthians 1:3,4

Two things to consider:

- We mentor another from our own experience of being mentored by God. As we experience God's "alongsideness" in our up's and down's, joys and sorrows, we can more naturally share His overflow with someone who is where we have been.

"God comes alongside us when we go through hard times..."

- We mentor another by getting close enough so that mutual vulnerability is natural and trusted. Authenticity is the vanguard of artless discipleship.

"...He brings us alongside someone else who is going through hard times so that we can be there for that person just a God was there for us."

You don't need a table to be a Table Mentor. You do need an ongoing relationship with the Ultimate Mentor, and a bold desire to get close to someone who needs to hear what you've learned.

~~

What Mentors Say:

"What do you love about mentoring?"

Wisdom, life experience, encouragement, and life together.
–Brittany

Seeing another person reason through her own solutions using the Bible as reference. Learning how to apply the Bible practically for others and myself. The increased connection and closeness when collaborating on people's issues, hearing them empathetically, and being very transparent with one another.
–Janelle

Seeing the Holy Spirit bring up discussions you never planned on, take you places you never dreamed up and watching fruit arise in both you and your mentee in ways you never saw coming. Gaining new perspectives. Remembering what it was like to be a new babe in Christ--how quickly we old Christians forget and how good for us to remember how a newborn babe in Christ thinks. The zeal of a new believer is contagious and inspiring. Growth in both people take place in mentoring.

–Melody H.

Being stretched and encouraged to grow.

–Suzanne

~~

Points to Ponder

- Do I know God better this year more than last?

- Have I seen His hand at work in and through my circumstances?

- Do I know someone well enough to share some of my hard places with her so that she can know how God can also be her strength?

Blessed to Be a Blessing

Both riches and honor come from you, and you rule over all. In your hand are power and might, and in your hand it is to make great and to give strength to all. And now we thank you, our God, and praise your glorious name. But who am I, and what is my people, that we should be able thus to offer willingly? For all things come from you, and of your own have we given you.

I Chronicles 29:12

Praying Alongside

"Lord, thanks for coming alongside of me. Please show me how you want me to come alongside another. May I offer what You've offered me. Thank You and Amen."

2

Why Mentor?

Are you already in a conversation with the Great Mentor: "Why me, Lord? Why should I mentor?"

If so, your dialogue may go something like this:

"Not sure why I'm reading this book, Lord."
"Don't you have enough people to do this?"
"Too daunting—sorry."
"I'm not really the type."
"Who would want me to tell them anything? I mean, look at my life--not exactly perfect. You know that more than anyone!"
"And besides, I'm shy (I'm busy, I'm tired, I'm ignorant of Scripture, I don't know anyone who wants what I know, I'm not an expert, I'm not mature enough, I need a mentor myself!")

I'll grant you that last one. We all need a mentor. But at the same time, we need to mentor.

Notice it's not really a dialogue. We just keep talking while God waits. When we finally let it rest, we may hear this:

- "You're reading it because I've been nudging you."
- "There are never enough people to mentor people – see My Word here:
  'The harvest is plentiful, but the laborers are few.'"
                                                    -Luke 10:2
- "Of course it's daunting. You wouldn't need Me if it weren't."
- "If you're Mine, you're the type. What's 'type' got to do with it, btw?"
- "I've got the perfect person in mind for you to meet with. Just waiting for you. (*Who* is not your problem.)"
- "All those "I's" – *I'm shy, busy, tired, ignorant*. That's why you have Me. And yes, you need a mentor, too. Have you asked anyone?"

So why mentor?

First and foremost, God says. Second, and almost as foremost, we aren't meant to journey alone.

Paul wrote:

Older women likewise are to be reverent in behavior, not slanderers or slaves to much wine. They are to teach what is good, and so train the young women to love their husbands and children, to be self-controlled, pure, working at home, kind, and submissive to their own husbands, that the word of God may not be reviled.

                                                    Titus 2:3-5 ESV

 Read these words again:

"Older women…they are to teach…and so train the young women…" I know. You don't feel old. You may be insulted to be called "old." But the truth is everyone is older than someone else. You may be younger than I am, but there is someone you know that is younger than you are.

Besides we are all going to be older say, by lunch.

So get over the obstacle of who you think you are: forever young – and revel in the fact that you are no longer in Junior High. Praising God along with you this very minute.

So God says, "Teach and train the younger." It's not a suggestion. That's first and foremost why we mentor.

Secondly, we need each other.

One morning, after saying goodbye to most of my coffee guests, I quietly mentioned to Liz: "Can you stay a little bit longer?"

I needed to talk. I knew Liz would listen without judging, and provide some solid wisdom. I didn't need to say much, nor did she. But I won't forget what she said and how she said it.

I needed mentoring. I'm old, but Liz is even older! (I'm sure she doesn't mind that I say that about her! Ha! She's raised five boys. I'm surprised she's not dead.)

So I asked her for help and she gave it graciously. That morning I was the mentee and she was the mentor. And she comes over for tea whenever she's invited.

We mentor and get mentored because we need each other.
As Solomon wisely noted:

Two are better than one, because they have a good reward for their toil. For if they fall, one will lift up his fellow. But woe to him who is alone when he falls and has not another to lift him up! Again, if two lie together, they keep warm, but how can one keep warm alone? And though a man might prevail against one who is alone, two will withstand him—a threefold cord is not quickly broken.

Ecclesiastes 4:9-12

Read these words again: "Two are better than one…if they fall, one will lift up his fellow…a threefold cord is not quickly broken."

We need each other to break our fall. We need each other to lift and encourage and to keep from becoming more broken than we already are.

Those are two simple reasons why we must mentor. To obey God (He knows what's good for us.) To help each other (often, another older, wiser woman knows what's good for us and God gives us insight on how to help another.)

Those two are the main dish – but here's the dessert!

When we mentor, we get so much joy in watching another flourish.
When we mentor, we pass on the legacy of God's faithfulness to us.
When we mentor, we get so many more "children" than we may already have.
When we mentor, we receive personal fulfillment from duplicating our walk with God into another's life.

And here's the frosting on that dessert:

When we mentor, God keeps us on our toes with Him—we can't authentically mentor without being authentic.

Wayne Anderson said:
> *Ministry is spillage.*

What's that mean to you?

Here's what it means to me: I can't give God out to others if I'm not filled up with God myself. Yes, I could fake it awhile. But I'll run out. The jar will run dry. I will burn out. Just as children learn more from what is caught than taught, our mentees will see that what is real to us, can be real to them when we are filled up to the brim with Him.

Here's the point: I don't have anything worth passing on to another if I'm not regularly working on my personal relationship with God.

When I pour into another, I need to be sitting at Jesus' feet on a regular basis.

The benefit of accountability is clear in business, family and all kinds of relationships. When we mentor another, we are kept accountable to what God is teaching us. For that reason alone, it's time to get started.

~~

What Mentors Say:

"What do you love about mentoring?"

I love finding the pulse of how God is working in the life of another.

–Brittany

I love relationships. I especially love to talk about the Lord and His Word with others. He is all about relationships and I love to watch "A-ha moments" as His Word brings new insight and understanding. Then in a longer mentoring relationship you get to see that go further into transformation.

–Laurie

I love watching someone grow and claim the same joys and victories, and answers to life as I have found. Mentoring helps me make sure that my challenges and instructions and lessons line up with my life.

–Mabel

~~

Points to Ponder

- Are you in a dialogue with God about becoming a mentor or a mentee?

- What makes you hesitate? Use the space below to write out your thoughts and lay them before the Lord.

- What appeals to you about mentoring someone?

Blessed to Be a Blessing

But we have this treasure in jars of clay, to show that the surpassing power belongs to God and not to us.

I Corinthians 4:7 ESV

Praying Alongside

"Lord, please fill me up with all of You so that when I get bumped, it's You that spills over into another's life. Give me a heart devoted You, 24/7. Thank You and Amen."

3

The Mentor & the Mentee

Who should mentor? You?
Who should be mentored? You?

Yes and yes.

Why the first "yes?" You are uniquely qualified to mentor another because your life experience, lessons, growth, family and education are uniquely yours. As much as I like to say, "That happened to me, too. I'm just like you!" I'm really not. And you are not like me.

That's a comfort and a miracle.

A comfort because we need to know we are special, especially created by God in the womb with our own stamp of nothing-like-it-except-for-her. She's the one and only one! One of life's basic needs is "significance" and God made it so from the very beginning. Here's why we are significant:

For you formed my inward parts;
you knitted me together in my mother's womb.
I praise you, for I am fearfully and wonderfully made.
Wonderful are your works;
my soul knows it very well.

Psalm 139:13,14

A snowflake, a fingerprint, and you—all miraculous. It's a miracle that God made so much variety. No two alike. That's why you can mentor—pass on to another—your unique journey with God, and He will be pleased as punch when you do.

Others may know more than I do on a given subject, but only I know what I know. And God may want me to give that slice of knowledge to someone in need. Granted, it may only be a slice, but He brings fruit from the smaller endeavor, and I'm grateful.

My brother Steve is an excellent guitar player and he knows how to teach it and teach it well to anyone willing to listen, learn and practice. However, he might remember that he isn't the highest paid guitar player in the world, nor the most famous and thus, never hang out his shingle and share his talent and expertise. Thankfully, he knows that when he teaches, people get excited and go on to become excellent musicians. He knows himself and gives accordingly.

Only this morning I read an excellent article on hospitality. I might know a bit about that topic, but I'm not the only one who does! (Just ask Martha Stewart!) I could say, "I'm not the expert, so I can't teach someone else what I know." Comparisons trap us inside our insecurities and keep us from mentoring when we get the opportunity.

Paul said we are to have an accurate view of ourselves and that includes our strengths and weaknesses. He knew he wasn't the best and he knew he wasn't the worst, but he felt compelled to share Christ day in and day out and we can feel the same.

For if I preach the gospel, that gives me no ground for boasting. For necessity is laid upon me. Woe to me if I do not preach the gospel!
I Corinthians 9:16 ESV

No boast, just fact. Our boast is in God and how He is growing us. That kind of confidence and humility makes a great mentor.

So besides your uniqueness among millions, your confidence in God, and your humility before God, what does it take to be a great mentor?

A growing relationship with Jesus Christ.

That's it. That's the main thing.

I didn't say a perfect relationship or sinless existence. Perfection and sinlessness is for later on when none of us will need to mentor or be mentored.

But qualified mentoring does take a *pressing on* mentality. *Pressing on* to know and love Christ better and deeper. As Paul, again the model mentor, cried out passionately to the Philippians:

Not that I have already obtained this or am already perfect, but I press on to make it my own, because Christ Jesus has made me his own. Brothers, I do not consider that I have made it my own. But one thing I do: forgetting what lies behind and straining forward to what lies ahead, I press on toward the goal for the prize of the upward call of God in Christ Jesus.

Let those of us who are mature think this way, and if in anything you think otherwise, God will reveal that also to you.
Philippians 3:f1f2-16 ESV

Paul put himself in the mature camp, but he knew he needed to keep pressing. And he did. "I press on to make it my own." To mentor well means we keep on pressing to make our relationship with God our own. We share our own stories, our walk with Christ, our own victories and losses and pressings to know and love Him more. That's all. A going-on-with-God til He comes or we go.

Yesterday a conference director called about the possibility of my speaking and she asked me: "Tell me when you first fell in love with Jesus. When did He grip your heart?" She went on: "Tell me how He is entering your world right now and making a difference in your life?"

Both great questions and I loved answering them. I know I love Jesus more today than fifty years ago, but that's when it started. I can tell you right now how He's leading and training and teaching and loving me. Today. Right now. He keeps after me, and, by His mercy and grace, I'm keeping after Him. Not perfectly. I'm not finished loving Him. He still has mounds of work to do in me. But He doesn't want me to wait til Glory to share my walk with Him alongside another.

Same with you.

If you feel God leading you to mentor, ask yourself:

- Do I love Jesus more today than ten years ago? One year ago?

- Do I trust Him for the unknowns in my future?

- Do I know some of His promises in His Word?

- Do I live like I trust in those promises?

If you answered: "Sort of. I'm working on it." You are ready to mentor. Paul wasn't perfect, just pressing.

If you think you know everything, think again.

If you know one promise in God's Word, you are ready to mentor that one promise. Ask God for someone to share it with today.

As for the second "Yes" – Yes, you should be mentored. We all need someone older and wiser in our lives. Even Star Wars got that right. We need a Yoda (Yodette?) who is wise in the Word.

Several years ago I got stuck on what a certain passage of Scripture meant. I knew someone who knew more than I did (she still does!) and I called her. Laurie came over with books and commentaries and handwritten notes. Amazing! So helpful! I had no idea how much she liked to do research. I said that very day, "Will you meet with me on a regular basis?" And she said, "Yes." That was about twenty years ago and we are having lunch next Tuesday, again.

I love having Laurie in my life. I want to be mentored for the rest of my days on earth. We don't meet as regularly as we did early on. But I can email or text her any time of day or night and we get together for lunch or breakfast as much as we can. It helps that I make her laugh, but she helps me when I'm laughing or crying because she always points me back to God. Should you have a mentor in your life? You bet. There is always someone older than you in the faith who is dying to share what they know. You will be a blessing to that someone as well, as they recount the faithfulness of God through their many years of walking with Him.

*For a list of "Attributes of a Mentor and Mentee," see pages 72 and 73 in Appendix.

~~

What the Mentee Says:

"What do you love about being mentored?"

Learning from a wise, discerning woman who loves the Lord.

—Emily

Unconditional love, challenge, and support.

—Carly

How crucial mentoring is in my life! Though I just went through one of the roughest seasons in my life (if not, the roughest), I never felt unloved or anxious about events because of the women I met with on a constant basis. Praise the Lord for bringing them into my life when I most needed them - in a new town, a new relationship status, and a new career!

—Jenny

I love having someone that I can be weak with – warts and all. Someone I can cry with and they will never judge me and always direct me to the Savior.

—Sue

Points to Ponder

- Do I compare myself too much to other "expert Christians" so that I don't feel worthy to mentor someone else?

- Am I confident in God's ability to use me, weak as I am?

- Will I begin today to ask God for a godly woman to come alongside and mentor me?

Blessed to Be a Blessing

May the Lord lead your hearts into a full understanding and expression of the love of God and the patient endurance that comes from Christ.
II Thessalonians 3:5

Praying Alongside

"Lord, may I never stop growing up in You. Help me faithfully seek Your face and Your holiness, and not compare myself to others. Thank You and Amen."

4
Finding the Right Match

You might wonder how you will find the right mentoring match. If someone comes your way, you may think:

How do I know I should mentor her?
How will I know she would be a good mentor for me?

God's got the relationships ready to go. Seeds have been planted. Hearts are being prepared. He does the real work, we just need to be open—an open heart and an open ear.

We need an open heart to receive God's right person right now. Get your antennae up and adjusted so that you're alert and ready. That may take a heart adjustment first:

- Am I submitted to the Holy Spirit on a daily basis so that I share the truth in love?

- Am I ready to live a transparent faith in order to help another grow up in Jesus?

"...speaking the truth in love, we are to grow up in every way into him who is the head, into Christ..."

Ephesians 4:15 ESV

We need open ears to move ahead when God says "move." That may need some hearing adjustment:

- Do I know when God is speaking to me?
- Am I willing to obey when I hear His voice?
- Will I allow God to clean out any distractions, sin, worries or fears so that I hear accurately?
- And will I ask Him with joy and expectation: "What is your will for me today, Lord?"
- Can I say along with young Samuel? "Speak, Lord, for your servant hears."

And the LORD came and stood, calling as at other times, "Samuel! Samuel!" And Samuel said, "Speak, for your servant hears."

I Samuel 3:10 ESV

I want to be open to God when He calls—open heart and open ears. It doesn't help to ask the Lord for guidance if I don't have a heart of obedience already in place.

Do you mentor everyone you meet today? I don't think so.

We stay close to the Shepherd so we'll know who to shepherd. We continue growing in Jesus to become the person God wants us to become.

I don't mentor every young woman who comes into my life. Nor do I think I should mentor every young woman who asks. It's an individual decision for me and I've not always been wise about becoming a mentor nor being mentored.

When I was first married, I was looking for help (isn't every new bride?) I met Joan at church and was impressed with her sweet spirit and love for the Lord. I asked her to begin meeting with me before I really knew her.

Big mistake!

Almost before we got going, I sensed that I couldn't respect her interpretation of Scripture nor the way she related to her husband. I didn't want to become who she had become. Now that's a red flag! Somehow I managed to gracefully remove myself from the mentor/mentee relationship that I had started. (Lord, forgive my impulsiveness!) but it was a good lesson, which I pass on to you:

- Know the person fairly well before committing to a long-term relationship.
- Take your time.
- Pray before you invite.

If you're interested in getting to know her better, get together casually first to see if she's one from whom you want to learn. Watch her from afar and up close: How does she view Scripture? How does she relate to her husband? Other women? Her children? Her church? And if possible, observe how she deals with conflict, personal disappointment, or job challenges. Think of some good "interview" questions so that you get to know her thoughts on areas in which you want to grow. For example, ask her:

What has caused you to grow most as a believer in the last year?

What is most challenging in your extended family relationships?

How do you keep your marriage fresh and alive?

How do you deal with anger or disappointment?

Do you ever question your faith?

No one is perfect and that's not what I'm saying. I am saying I jumped in too quickly and I was more careful the next time. When you ask a probing question, you can receive insight needed to make a wise decision.

The mentoring relationships that have worked longest and best are based on love, support and honest sharing. I might go so far as to say they are best when you're both members of a "mutual admiration society." You simply like each other to begin with, and you find yourself comfortable sharing your vulnerabilities, hopes and dreams.

As Scripture says:

And, above everything else, be truly loving, for love is the golden chain of all the virtues.

Colossians 3:14 Phillips

You may know you are ready to pour God's love on to another person, but you are wondering what is the best way to find that person.

Which works best: an organic almost accidental meet-up and mentor, or following a program that's planned with great intention?

Either can be great. Either can be used by God.

The formal program can work. I've been "assigned" to certain women with particular needs and I'm always willing to share what I know about growing up in Christ, but usually they turn out to be more short-term. Once an issue is addressed and worked on together, often the mentee is ready to move on to something or someone else. Or in some cases, I'm thinking I'm not the right person to help them move forward. Either way, I learn from that person and from that experience and most of all I come to know and love a fellow sister.

I met Lois through such a program and learned that even though she had made some poor choices in the past—as we all have—she was ready to move on and grow in her knowledge of God and Scripture. We met for twelve weeks and she flourished. I knew at that point that another woman might be just the ticket to help her continue to progress. And they are still meeting! So exciting!

I've found mentors and mentees by doing what I like to do: inviting friends and strangers over for coffee. When sharing around the table, you find kindred minds and hearts, which often turn into times of ongoing mentoring relationships.

I met my neighbor, Cassie, at my annual neighborhood Christmas coffees. She always stayed longer to chat. Finally I asked if she'd like to get together one-on-one and she said, "Yes!" I knew it was an open opportunity that I should not ignore. She's a new mom, and her own mother had died a few years back. Though we don't meet regularly--as on the same day, same time sort of thing--we are close enough locationally to meet up on any given day or time. We just text to see if either are available and go from there.

My friend, Jean has described these organic meet–up's like this: "Sue brings women together at her table, and then sends them on their way with new friends and connections. I just happened to stay."

And I'm so glad she did. Jean and I have been friends now for years and it's often mutual mentorship as we pray for and support one another through the evolving parenting stages. Praise God for those who stay. It's all in God's plan.

What Mentors Say:

"How did you find your mentee?"

Mostly through small group relationships.

—Suzanne

The family pastor assigned me to her. The other one I was sitting next to at a mentoring night from Grace Church.

—Ceslie

I don't look for them directly. Sometimes people ask me and other times I just ask someone to coffee because I see that they need encouragement. What develops or continues is what God determines.

—Gretchen

God brought her to me, literally. Met at church, invited her to our growth group.

—Brittany

My mentors were not actually "assigned" or "organized" to be my mentor. The Lord just kept putting people in my life that were brave enough to follow the Lord's prompting to help me in my walk with the Lord and to positively critique my life and walk so that I could grow...and so I followed that same pattern: just be conscious of the Lord's prompting to do the same for others as had been done for me.

—Mabel

~~

What Mentees Say:

"How did you find your mentor?"

Through a home Bible Study

–Melody H.

I asked her.

–Carly

I saw something in another woman and asked her to share with me how God worked in her life.

–Melody C.

One saw a common desire to know and serve God so we just set it up.

–Laurie

She found me.

–Brittany

By listening and praying for the right relationship to present itself.

–Suzanne

~~

Points to Ponder

- Am I ready to pour my life into another's?

- Have I counted the cost of time and energy?

- Am I plugged into God's Word so that what I share will be truth?

Blessed to Be a Blessing

Trust in the Lord with all your heart, and do not lean on your own understanding.
In all your ways acknowledge him, and he will make straight your paths.

Proverbs 3:5,6 ESV

Praying Alongside

"Lord, help me know the person You have picked out for me to mentor and to be mentored by. May I follow Your leading. I need discernment and wisdom. Thank You and Amen."

5

Time & Place

What's best in structuring your mentoring relationship? Once begun is there no end til Glory? You may never mentor if you hear Buzz Lightyear's voice buzzing in your ears: "You will mentor from infinity to beyond!"

Yikes! If so, I might never begin.

There are two basic mentor structures:

- A formal time frame
- A beginning with no real end in sight (more like Buzz but with the Holy Spirit in control)

If you are new to the person or new to mentoring, I suggest you begin with the formal time frame. I usually set up a three month plan, twice a month.

Why?

After three months—

- you will know if the relationship is working—a match or not?
- you both can evaluate the value of your time together
- you can decide: are you reaching goals and meeting a need?

I like putting something on the calendar. It doesn't matter what kind of calendar, what matters is the plan. If I write or note it somewhere, it's far more likely to happen.

When Grace announced she was going back to work part time, we knew we could no longer enjoy spontaneous lunches and brunches. She wailed: "I'll miss you guys so much!" Three friends and I had been meeting together for years – sharing and praying and crying and laughing and eating. Our mutual-mentoring was breaking bread the way it was meant to be broken. But now the reality of work seemed to be breaking up the pack.

But it didn't need to.

I walked into my kitchen, grabbed a pencil and stood in front of the refrigerator door calendar. (This was in the days of refrigerator door calendars.) "Grace, what days will you be working?" I asked, "Let's set a date for next month and we can still meet."

That day we set dates for the next four months, one day for each of us to host a simple meal. And we kept meeting. In fact, because Grace needed the structure to fit in with her new work-schedule, we met with even more intention.

Here's a good encouragement: Your job and family and normal life constraints can work in your favor as you choose mentoring as a priority and intentionally fit it into your schedule. Sometimes, the busier we are, the more we can accomplish. We always have time to do what we really want to do. But placing it on the calendar helps make that happen.

I make my formal mentoring meetings twice a month due to my other commitments, but some prefer once a week. And be sure to ask your mentee: Are you ready to make this time together a commitment? Write it down and seal it with prayer. Life happens, of course, but it's good to talk through the challenges of adding mentoring to that life. It may help you, too, to ask another friend to commit to pray for you as you mentor another.

It's up to you whether you meet on a weeknight or early Saturday morning. Some young moms love to be treated to Starbucks when their husbands can watch the kids. Others prefer a walk or hike while talking and tackling tough subjects like marriage and child raising or addressing the age-old question: Is it safe to trust God or not?

I've been mentored at the lunch table, the coffee shop, the local favorite Chinese restaurant, the couch and the back porch. The geographical place doesn't matter; the place on the calendar does.

Tip: restaurants are not always the best due to the normal interruptions by servers and placing an order or background noise.
Coffee shops work better.
Home at your table works best.
Time limits are up to you. If I go to someone's home, I can more easily set a limit. "Whoops! Looks like I'll need to run." If you don't need to worry about going too long, then don't. But it's good to have that discussion up front.

When I know I will meet with a new friend for three months to begin with, at the end of that time, I feel the freedom to bow out of the formal mentoring relationship in a graceful manner, no feelings hurt. To develop a gracious exit is a valuable tool. Jesus used it more than once:

But Jesus Himself would often slip away to the wilderness and pray.
Luke 5:16, NASB

If you have expectations more or less in place, "slipping away" results in a good thing for both parties.

With my less structured mentoring relationships, there's no need to worry about times and places. I am a busy person. You are, too. That word 'busy' is becoming a by-word for not taking care of yourself and not being wise. It could be, but it doesn't have to be.

Some of us like being busy, but I only want to be as busy as God wants me to be. Time constraints and accountability helps me gauge God's desires for me on any given day or week.

I begin my day with this:

Good morning, Lord. Help Yourself – to me, to my day, to whatever you've given me to do.

And then I do the next thing. Some days are busier than others. But with that start-up-surrender to God of my day, mind and heart--my days don't need to be frazzled. And when I do become frazzled, I return to my prayer:

"Lord, help Yourself. I'm Yours."

We need to evaluate how busy we should be. What fits into that busyness? And what does God want us to do with our time?

My favorite expression lately has been:

"My To-Do List becomes my To-Be List when I make God first on my list".

My list looks like this:
- Relate Well With God
- Everything Else

When you make your list the same, you will know when and where and how long each mentoring relationship should be.

I love how this college gal started her day:

Good Morning, God. This is Margaret, reporting for duty!

Take a cue from Margaret. Give yourself and your day to Jesus daily, and trust Him to make good daily decisions. And it's something for which you can keep each other accountable. Try it for yourself, and it could be the most important lesson you pass on to your mentee.

Good Morning, Lord. This is _____, reporting for duty, expecting your guidance, and enjoying your love. Amen.

When asked, "What's your biggest mentoring challenge?" most often the answer was: time. How can I fit it into an already busy life?

That's where surrender to God's prioritizing kicks in, as well as learning to listen well to the Spirit's prompting. And then, putting it on the calendar. Like this:

Surrender (to God)
Listen (to the Spirit)
Place (on the calendar)

This season may not be your season. But don't let that keep you from asking God if He wants you to ask someone to meet with you—to pour your life into and to be poured into. And when would He like you to start.

But seek first the kingdom of God and his righteousness, and all these things will be added to you.

Matthew 6:33 ESV

~~

What Mentors Say:

"What's the biggest challenge and what made it successful?"

The greatest challenge is finding the time.

–Melody C.

We set up the dates for six months on my calendar so I would remember to do it.

–Ceslie

The greatest challenge is finding a time that works. My mentor was incredibly flexible and would come to me sometimes and even bring breakfast because she knew I had "littles" at home and it was harder for me to get out. Other times we would meet at a restaurant.

–Melody H.

Spending consistent time and being willing to be vulnerable and transparent.

–Suzanne

The biggest challenge is life and its time constraints.

–Laurie

When Christiane asked me to mentor her I told her I could meet with her on occasion on a Saturday morning. Not putting it on the calendar made our relationship a little too fluid – as in, we forgot to meet! Especially since she had baby #2. Life is more fluid with babies, in general! But we still reach out to each other and pick up where we left off. When Maren approached me, I said the same thing, but it turned out she just wanted some counsel on a specific topic. So we met one time, and we check in with each other every once in a while.

–Sue

~ ~

Points to Ponder

- Can you say with Margaret: "Whatever you want me to do today, Lord, I'm ready" (including placing mentoring on my calendar.)

- With your current schedule, would mentoring work best twice a month or every other month?

- Would it help to go over your current schedule with a trusted friend and ask for her input as you consider coming alongside another?

Blessed to Be a Blessing

For everything there is a season, and a time for every matter under heaven...He has made everything beautiful in its time...There is a time and a way for everything..."

Ecclesiastes 3:1,11; 8:6

Praying Alongside

"Lord, may I completely surrender my life to You. Show me how to arrange my days, hours and minutes so that I grow and help another to grow in You. Thank You and Amen."

6
What to Talk About

If you're an extrovert, you may not even consider that a problem—because it isn't! At least you know you can fill up any silent spaces. But of course, mentoring doesn't have to do with being an extrovert or an introvert because it's usually a one-on-one relationship. And some of my introverted friends are the biggest talkers I know. (Make sure your coffee pot is full!)

You may be hesitant to enter a mentoring relationship, however, it may only be because you don't know where to start and what to share.

I always begin by asking:

"What would you like to get out of our time together?"

Some gals are very specific and others have no idea; they just like you or they're desperate for adult fellowship! Go ahead and ask this first question and then ask some getting-to-know-you questions because that's what you want to do—get to know one another for the sake of helping her grow up in Jesus.

Questions like:

- Where are you from?
- Describe your family of origin.
- How long have you been in a relationship with God?
- What are your biggest joys and your biggest challenges currently?
- Are there specific changes you would like to make in your life?
- Where do you see yourself in the next five years?
- Have you been mentored before; if so, how was it helpful?
- What is your understanding of a mentor-mentee relationship?

Often, one question leads to another and you're on your way to becoming acquainted. Questions also help you both determine the kind of mentoring that needs to occur.

The most important aspect of mentoring is strengthening another's walk with God. Make that the focus of each time together. Even ask your mentee for feedback on occasion:

Do you see growth since we've begun meeting?
Is there something you want to change about our time together?
Do we need to emphasize more on_____?

Giving her permission give input into your times together will help her take ownership of her progress and deepen your intimacy together.

Formal and Informal Mentoring

If your gal simply wants to be accountable in her spiritual growth, there are many books that you can study together. Books are good because then you don't have to feel like you are the expert! I am not a seminary grad, and I studied the Bible in a classroom setting many (many) years ago. That fact could intimidate me and keep me from coming alongside anyone. But if I have a solid Bible study book at my disposal, I'm confident in learning along with my mentee and I can trust that I'm not hindering her growth.

Some of my favorites I've used are any studies by Cynthia Heald, Kelly Minter, Priscilla Shirer, Beth Moore, Linda Dillow, and Carole Mayhall. Ask your friends or your mentor which ones they've used and enjoyed. Even if you don't finish the book by the time your set schedule is completed, you both could continue on your own, and possibly meet up one last time once you've both finished.

You may find that your gal only needs to get out of the house, drink a cup of coffee and talk about her challenges that week. That is a totally worthy way to go. Sometimes we don't need one more study to complete. Even so, prayer and Scripture memory can be part of your relationship.

Sometimes a woman's issues are more difficult and weighty than you can or should handle. If you find yourself in discussions that make you feel either uncomfortable or are more serious in nature than you have experienced, always refer to a professional counselor, therapist and or/pastor. Our church has more than one trained counselor on staff, which is a great place to start. A mentoring relationship is not a therapist relationship—unless, of course, you are a therapist. If you have any doubts about continuing to meet with someone who is in a deep predicament, that is God talking to you. Listen to Him. Explain your views to your mentee, offer to help set up an appointment with another person—even offer to accompany her to the first session. And don't feel guilty about it. (Do you need to read that again? And don't feel guilty about it – as if you've failed.) Maybe she would only seek professional help by starting to meet with you. So God used you, even if for a short while. If we continue to hold onto a relationship which He is telling us to stop, it's unhealthy for both, and it can be a red flag that we have all waved at one time or another that says: "I'm the only one who can help this person!"

That flag has tripped me up more than once. I love what my dear friend, Bonnie told me years ago: "Sue, God is the One Who does the real work anyway." So true. So right. So move on, dear one and He will do what He does best: grow us up into the image of His Son, in His way and by His plan.

When I begin to mentor a new friend, I begin by introducing a Personal Growth Plan. It's simple, mentee-led, and a foolproof way to get things rolling. Feel free to copy what I do to the letter and then alter it along the way to fit your style and the needs of your mentee. A copy is under Worksheets at the back of this book, and a full-page size can be downloaded at: welcomeheart.com/book-free-printables.

At our first time together, I present the Personal Growth Plan and assign it as homework to complete for our next meeting time. Take time to go over it and suggest some avenues for growth, if need be.

If she has difficulty deciding how and where to grow, fill out one for yourself first and keep each other accountable. That might be a first step in mutual vulnerability which builds trust and confidence between you both. In regards to the Growth Plan, your role as Mentor is three-fold:

- Help her decide on goals and strategies to reach her goals

- Encourage manageable and attainable goals (remind her that you can't change everything in three months!)

- Check in regularly as her accountability partner—that's why you're in her life

Setting up a Growth Plan with someone will give direction to your time together and it helps answer the question: "What do we do when we meet?!" Also it will help keep your time together on track. When we check in on our plan each week, it can help solve a potential problem of talking too long on personal issues. We want to be good and compassionate listeners, but you as her mentor can't solve all her problems. As you check progress that she has charted out, she's reminded that God's greatest desire for her is her relationship with Himself. And you are in her life to help her re-focus on the One who knows and loves her best.

I've started with this plan every time. Be sure to check the Worksheets section to find a link to download this worksheet, as well as nine other worksheets to help you as you mentor.

Personal Growth Plan

What are your goals in these areas:

Spiritual-
Family-
Marriage-
Personal-
Relationships (other than family)-
Financial-
Ministry-
Physical-
Career-
Community Outreach-
Educational-
Option to add your own: _____

Not all of the above need apply. If it's too much to handle, let her pick her top three areas of desired growth. Or she can divide up the category. For instance, under *Family* she can set goals in her relationships with her siblings, her children, her mother-in-law.

(That's always a good one!) Or under *Marriage* she can work on specific areas like: time alone as a couple, building up my spouse, conflict-resolution. Under *Personal* she could list: thinking before speaking, building an attitude of gratitude, choosing joy. Don't worry if some goals seem to overlap. The point is to get her thinking about progressing towards knowing God better and displaying His glory as His child.

Then add the time frame:

3-Month Goals-
1-Year Goals-
5 (or 10)-Year Goals-
Lifetime Goals-

Strategies to Reach Goals

Then add the strategies she will implement to reach those goals. This could take more than one meeting and more than one page!

Your job as mentor will include a two-fold responsibility:

- To help your mentee to form her desires into measurable and attainable goals;

- To keep her accountable to her growth plan.

Before you send her on her way with high hopes to change the world—hers and that of all those she loves—discuss the difference between Goals vs. Desires. I learned this helpful distinction from Christian psychologist/author Larry Crabb.

Goals are dependent upon you--things that you have the power to change.

Desires are dependent upon another person.

As much as we think we might, we really don't have the power to change another person. That may be the biggest wake-up call that you teach your mentee.

For example: my goal may be to have a great relationship with my adult daughter but that is dependent on her as well as myself. So I should make that a *desire*, not a *goal*. My desire is to have a growing and great relationship, but I only have control over what I do to make that relationship great. So I ask my daughter: "What do you want from me to make our relationship better?" How she answers that question, I can add to my goals list because it's something that I have control over. That is a valuable and vulnerable question. But if we want growth, we may need to ask it. And it may be the best step in helping reach that desire of a great relationship.

I may desire my high school son to grow in his faith. And I can provide all he could use to do so. But I can't make his spiritual growth my *goal*. That will be up to him. It's my *desire* that he makes great strides. I pray that he will, but I can't list it under my family goals. See the difference? Instead, my goal might be to be to get to know my son better, to encourage him in how God has made him, and to set the stage for his spiritual growth. As a strategy, Laurie would ask godly college students to take her kids to breakfast, and she paid the bill. She did what she could to help her kids by surrounding them with godly mentors, but their personal growth was up to them.

Why make a big deal of this distinction?

Most of our frustration (read: anger) comes from making our *desires* into *goals*, and we just don't have that kind of power. We do all we can on our end and leave the results up to God. I find when I think in those terms, I trust God more, I live in peace and joy, and I'm less annoying to the ones I love best.

This exercise may be the most that your first meeting can handle but the second half is as important as the first. It won't help to set goals without determining strategies to meet those goals. Discussing strategies could take more than one meeting and more than one piece of paper, but that doesn't matter.

For example, if her goal is to become a better Christian or to have more faith, you might need to help her decide what she could do to reach those goals. The strategies lists will be longer than the goals list and could be assigned the second week.

Your mentee may need your help with figuring out how to reach her goals. Part of the mentor's life experience can pour into an overly enthusiastic let's-change-the-world attitude and let's-do-it-right-now – and give wisdom where it's needed. Not to dampen her enthusiasm, just encouragement to go slow, take small bites, and gain small successes. Yes? Yes.

~~

What Mentors Say:

"What would you do differently next time?"

Ask early on how I could pray for her. Perhaps introduce a book or resource we could study together to keep us aligning on topic and with applicable Scripture references.

–Angela

Have intentional check-in conversations: How is this working? What would you change? Let's hear some feedback.

–Carly

I do everyone differently, but all must be focused on the Word and the Lord.

–Laurie

I used to think mentoring had to do with a book and accomplishing a desired goal, and while goals are great, I have found that to not be bound by these things is freeing and lets mentoring be what God wants it to be. To my younger mentoring self I'd say let go of what you think mentoring looks like and let the Spirit of God lead that relationship, all the while being built on truth and grace and love.

–Melody H.

~~

Points to Ponder

- Do I need to fill out a Personal Growth Plan first so I can see how it can be beneficial?

- Do I need a new journal? (I always love an excuse for a new journal)

- Do I understand the difference between goals and desires?

- Do I understand the difference between goals and the strategies to reach goals?

Blessed to Be a Blessing

Keep putting into practice all you learned and received from me—everything you heard from me and saw me doing. Then the God of peace will be with you.

Philippians 4:9 NLT

Praying Alongside

"Lord, please deepen my desire to grow up into all the fullness of You. Help me figure out specific areas that I need to work on, and show me how I can help another with how You are leading her. Thank You and Amen."

Afterword

Recently our church said "goodbye" to Jeff, one of our associate pastors. He was leaving to become a lead pastor after having been mentored by Tim, our lead pastor for several years. Tim spent years getting Jeff ready to lead his own flock, and off he went two weeks ago. Bittersweet. Joy and tears. But it happened as it should have. One Paul (Tim) pouring his life into his Timothy (Jeff) so that the church can grow and multiply.

It happened as it should have. We come alongside another to teach and train so that that one can also teach and train. And it's good for both.

In the words of Sherri Langton:

"Do you have a Timothy? If you do, you are blessed. If you don't, having one begins with availability. It deepens with investing yourself in that person. I have learned that it's impossible for a young one in the faith to 'keep on keeping on' without the support of a Paul. And I'm also beginning to think that it's impossible for a mature Christian to deepen his walk with God without a Timothy."

Wow. Those are big claims, but I think she's right. We all need a *Timothy*—someone to whom we come alongside to help deepen their walk with God. And we all need a *Paul* to help us "keep on keeping on." Blessings on you as you begin to walk closer to another, alongside, for the sake of gospel living and Christ-like growth. You and I are blessed to be a blessing. Ask God for someone to sit with at your table. Every table tells a story and the most important one we can tell is the story of God's pursuit of us from Creation to Redemption and life with Him eternally. And we are always...

Better together,

Sue Donaldson

Praying Alongside

"Lord, I pray alongside these women who want to obey and serve you by mentoring and being mentored. Give us humble and listening hearts. May Who You are to us spill over readily into the lives of others. We depend on You, every day in every way. Thank You and Amen."

Worksheets

Get started in this most wonderful of relationships—
Go to WelcomeHeart.com and download these ten
FREE printable worksheets:

welcomeheart.com/book-free-printables

1. Getting Started—Mentor Questionnaire

2. Personal Growth Plan

3. Inspiration for Mentors

4. Meeting Time

5. Praying Scripture

6. Characteristics of a Mature Believer

7. Quiet Time Inspiration, Part I

8. Quiet Time Inspiration, Part II

9. "Wonderful Things" –Tips for Bible Study

10. "Eyes on God" –Tips on Prayer

Getting Started – Mentor Questionnaire

- What do you hope to get out of our mentoring relationship?

- Have you been in a formal mentoring relationship before? As a mentor or mentee? How was it helpful to your spiritual growth?

- What will be a challenge to you to make a commitment to meet regularly and how can I be of help?

- What do you see as the biggest challenges in your walk with God currently?

- How would you like to see your relationship with Him change?

- Share your biggest strengths and one of your weaknesses.

- Whether or not you're a goal-setting type of person, are you willing to dig in and pray about making progress in areas that may need some change?

- Do I have your permission to keep you accountable to what you want to grow in?

- What could you use the MOST from me? Cheerleading? Prayer? Accountability? Teaching? A Bible study?

- How can I pray for you this week?

Next Meeting: When is the best time to contact you and how? Text? Email? Will you need a reminder?

Time--
Date--
Place--

Personal Growth Plan

Choose 3 or more areas of growth from the following list or add your own category:

Spiritual, Family, Financial, Physical, Educational, Career/Job, Building Community, Outreach, Talent Development, Service, Time-Management, Home, Marriage, Character, Recreation, Other_____

Part I – Goals: Answers the Question—Where Am I Going?

After deciding on what areas God is speaking to you about, determine some short-term and long-term goals. Divide them into 3-month or 6-month, 1-year or 5-year goals, and at least one Lifetime goal since we continue in process until Glory.

Example:

Spiritual—Putting God's Word in My Heart
3-month: Develop the habit of meeting with God every day
1-year: Apply a Scripture memory system
Lifetime: Love God's Word and live under it as a daily practice

Example:

Character—My Tongue
3-month: Become a better listener
1-year: Use my words to build up rather than tear down
Lifetime: Become a woman of discretion

Part II – Strategies:
Answers the Question—How Will I Get There?

Example:

Spiritual—Putting God's Word in My Heart

1. Create a quiet time area and basket of supplies
2. Ask others how they go about making time for God
3. Meet with Lorraine and learn her Scripture memory system
– apply it to my life

Example:

Character—My Tongue

1. Memorize a verse on the tongue – search Proverbs
2. Ask my husband what words from me would make him feel
loved and respected
3. Be accountable to my friends to stop words of complaint or gossip

Inspiration for Table Mentoring

"A woman of excellence is one who has found her security and worth in Jesus Christ. She does not need to look to people or things to feel loved or valued. She is now free to love and serve because she can trust her needs to be met by her Heavenly Father."

—Cynthia Heald

"No other single discipline is more useful and rewarding than memorizing Scripture. No other single exercise pays greater spiritual dividends. Your attitudes and outlook will begin to change. Your confidence and assurance will be enhanced. Your faith will be solidified."

—Charles Swindoll

"Get into the habit of saying, 'Speak, Lord,' and life will become a romance."

—Oswald Chambers

"God wants me to pray. The devil does not want me to pray, and does all he can to hinder me. He knows that we can accomplish more through our prayers than through our work. He would rather have us do anything else than pray."

—Unknown

"We needn't plead for God to fill our hearts with His love. He is waiting all around us, like love is pressing round us on all sides. Cease to resist and instantly love takes possession."

—Amy Carmichael

"Christ broke bread to distribute it easier. It's wonderful what God can do with a broken heart when you give Him all the pieces."

—J. Sidlow Baxter

"Don't seek to know your spiritual gifts as much as to seek to be God's gift to those around you."

—Dave Lomas

"Make your first priority to learn what is Jesus' first priority: love God and love your neighbor as yourself."

—Steve Leonard

"Our first and foremost task is faithfully to care for the inward fire so that when it is really needed it can offer warmth and light to lost travelers."

—Henri Nouwen

"'Blessed are the poor in spirit' literally means 'beggars in spirit,' i.e., 'Blessed are those who realize they don't have it all together and don't have all the answers.'"

—Wayne Anderson

"All of God's people are ordinary people who have been made extraordinary by the purpose he has given them."

—Oswald Chambers

Mentor Meeting Time

Session # _____

Date _____

- ❑ Open in prayer
- ❑ Growth plan check-in
- ❑ Scripture memory
- ❑ Bible lesson or workbook
- ❑ Since we met last:
- ❑ How is God growing you?
- ❑ Where have you seen His hand in your life?
- ❑ Do you need to adjust your Growth Plan? (Too much? Too little?)
- ❑ Have you shared your progress with a friend or family member?
- ❑ Is God speaking to you about something in particular?
- ❑ How can I be of encouragement to you today?

Prayer requests:

_____

Next meeting time and place:

_____

Praying Scripture

You can never go wrong with the Word. Pray these words enough and they will memorize you!

I keep asking that the God of our Lord Jesus Christ, the glorious Father, may give you the Spirit[a] of wisdom and revelation, so that you may know him better. I pray that the eyes of your heart may be enlightened in order that you may know the hope to which he has called you, the riches of his glorious inheritance in his holy people, and his incomparably great power for us who believe.

Ephesians 1:17-19a

I pray that out of his glorious riches he may strengthen you with power through his Spirit in your inner being, so that Christ may dwell in your hearts through faith. And I pray that you, being rooted and established in love, may have power, together with all the Lord's holy people, to grasp how wide and long and high and deep is the love of Christ, and to know this love that surpasses knowledge—that you may be filled to the measure of all the fullness of God.

Ephesians 3:16-19

And this is my prayer: that your love may abound more and more in knowledge and depth of insight, so that you may be able to discern what is best and may be pure and blameless for the day of Christ, filled with the fruit of righteousness that comes through Jesus Christ—to the glory and praise of God.

Philippians 1:9-11

For this reason, since the day we heard about you, we have not stopped praying for you. We continually ask God to fill you with the knowledge of his will through all the wisdom and understanding that the Spirit gives,[a so that you may live a life worthy of the Lord and please him in every way: bearing fruit in every good work, growing in the knowledge of God, being strengthened with all power according to his glorious might so that you may have great endurance and patience, and giving joyful thanks to the Father, who has qualified you[b] to share in the inheritance of his holy people in the kingdom of light.

Colossians 1:9-12

Hear me, Lord, and answer me, for I am poor and needy. Guard my life, for I am faithful to you; save your servant who trusts in You. You are my God; have mercy on me, Lord, for I call to You all day long. Bring joy to Your servant, Lord, for I put my trust in You. You, Lord, are forgiving and good, abounding in love to all who call to You. Hear my prayer, Lord; listen to my cry for mercy. When I am in distress, I call to You, because You answer me.

Psalm 86: 1-7

Marks of a Mature Believer

1. Growing up means not giving up. (Hebrews 12:1,2)

2. Growing up is displayed by a deepening dependence on God. (I Peter 5:7)

3. Growing up is a privilege expressed by obedience. (John 15:9,10)

4. A mature person continues to grow into the likeness of Jesus. (Philippians 3:12-14)

5. A mature believer surrenders herself to God, focusing on His greatness vs. focusing on people and events. (Isaiah 55:8,9)

6. A mature believer has a great memory: recalling God's faithfulness provides needed peace and strength for any present situation and the "unknowns" of the future. (Psalm 118: 21)

7. Growing up in Jesus means we care enough about our relationship with God to do something about it. (Ephesians 4:14,15)

8. The mark of a mature believer is someone who takes her lead from God's Word, first and foremost, and recognizes that obedience is a good thing (not a bad thing!) (II John 1:6)

9. A mature believer prays with an attitude of perfect trust and an eagerness to ask and to seek, remembering—"Why my Father knows all about it!" (Luke 11:15)

10. A mature believer shows compassion for another yet continually points them to Jesus as their ultimate source of comfort and strength. (Luke 12:7)

11. A mature believer draws closer to God in her painful circumstances rather than becoming bitter and distant from Him. (Psalm 145:18)

12. A mature believer can say with Paul: "Follow my example as I follow the example of Christ." (I Corinthians 11:1)

13. A mature believer recognizes her strength is in her poverty; she comes to God with empty hands, "Lord, I am poor in spirit." (II Corinthians 12:9,10)

Quiet Time Inspiration, Part I

Four roadblocks to spending time alone with God:

- Time– can't fit it in (you don't know the best time to meet with God)

- Tiredness– early morning or late at night? (bleary-eyed and overworked!)

- Toddlers– or any interruptions (my current one is a puppy!)

- Taste– the Word has become dry and tasteless (which weakens motivation.)

How to overcome the roadblocks:

Perspective— How we look at it makes all the difference

1. Ask God for a desire to spend time with Him – Psalm 42.

We want to hunger for God's Word rather than view our time together as just one more thing to tack onto an already full day.

Is our day run by the urgent vs. the expedient?

Often we do what needs doing in the moment rather than spending time with the One who knows how best to run our lives. Are we willing to surrender to Him first?

2. Ask God for His priorities.

We say we believe God is our main source of hope, strength and direction – but we don't do anything about drawing on that hope, strength and direction.

Is God my urgent?

My life's blood?

The air that I breathe?

If you believe that, you will be driven to the Word.

Is God my greatest love?

Our time with Him is a response to the Lover of my soul, rather a duty to a harsh taskmaster. God created us to relate to Him, and He longs for communion with us.

Is God my King?

Humility – What makes you think you can do this Christian life on your own strength? When we ignore time with God we must believe we don't need Him – or that we can power through.

Plan— How we work at it makes all the difference

The houseplants by my kitchen sink stay alive because they get my attention and get easily watered. What do you need to do to get God at your sink? Start with a commitment of 5 minutes a day. We can all fit in 5 minutes. Begin today. Here's how:

- Get a place—make it pretty and restful.
- Get a handled basket so that you can pick it up and move locations if need be.
- Get an accountability partner—and give her permission to check in on you.
- Get a verse—choose one on which to meditate throughout the day.

Tools for your basket: pen, paper, journal, Bible, devotional, notecards, candle, favorite coffee mug, and reading glasses if needed!

Make it fun, make it yours—but do make it! When everything is in one place, you are more likely to run to God on a regular basis.

Quiet Time Inspiration, Pt. II

"Rocking With Jesus"
A mother's intimate moments with her child reveal God's heart

My 2-year-old finds her place early on my lap. Chest to chest, her head and neck nestled close, legs astride my waist, serenely sucking her pacifier. Content just to sit quietly, rocking, resting, embracing. I blanket her with a pretty lap quilt, tucking in edges to block the morning air.

I'm learning anew to sit still before my Father. I feel like a 2-year old in this endeavor to lay my head in silence upon His breast. I hear "should's" echoing. I should have realized this sooner, done it for years, known its importance. Oh well, I'm doing it now. And how I need it. I didn't realize how much. No pleas, no confessions, no talking. Just communication of the deepest kind.

Finally a finger is lifted. "See?" I did see. A tiny stray fingernail. I brush it aside.
"Ok?"
"Ok." Her head returns to my shoulder. All's right again.

So typical when the silence is broken it's first to lift my hurt to You, Lord. "See?" I ask. I barely raise my hand. "Look, Jesus, I hurt. I think I'm bleeding." He looks deeply into my wound, shows me His, and hugs me tighter. I'm comforted.

First wonderings. "Where's Sissie?"
"Asleep," I whisper.
"Oh," she whispers back. "Where's Daddy?"
"At work."
"Oh."
Minutes pass. "Hold her."
"Your dollie?"
"Yes."
So room is made for dollie under the quilt. She gets tucks, too, to keep the comfort in.

So many questions and anxieties over those I love. "Do you know where they are? Will you keep them warm?"
He makes room for them as I hand my precious ones again into His care.

I settle in and remember Isaiah's picture:
"He gathers the lambs in His arms, and carries them close to His heart; He gently leads those that have young." (Isaiah 40:11)

Another finger pokes from the quilt. "See, Mommy?" This time a pen marking.

"Oh, sweetheart, writing goes only on paper, remember?"

"Uh, huh." Assured, she re-nestles.

Once I'm tucked in His love, I spill my slightest weakness, my deepest sin. I don't doubt His forgiveness. He is so gentle in His correction. Confession is good for my soul.

More rocking. More silence. Then sweet hands emerge, finding the lines of my mouth, my nose, my eyes, settling on my earlobes as the most interesting playthings. I invite her exploring touch. Then came another game. "Kiss my eyes,." I kiss her eyes, her hair, her nose.

Jesus says, "Come to Me, Sue, And keep coming and coming again and again and again." I'm not just invited once. I can explore Him freely, search His character, find His heart. I reach toward His face and find His head inclined my way. We trade kisses and I smile.

Quiet again, she notices my shift in the rocking movement. No longer up and down, we swivel back and forth. She takes exception.

"Hey!"

"It's okay. We just changed direction."

"Ok." She can handle that.

A few moments more of easy embracing. Then, "I want to play, mommy."

"Okay. Off you go. Have fun."

I, too, take exception when You change my course. "What's happening here?" I demand. I recall the disciples' determined resignation in face of the unknown, "Lord, where else would we go?" Where else, indeed! Plans alter, lives change, who knows the next day even? But today I've laid my head on Your chest and heard Your heartbeat. Secured by these moments of endearment and rocked in Your love, I'll go off to be Mommy, knowing I'm always Your child.

August 20, 1994 ~ with Bethany Anne

"Wonderful Things"
Tips for Beginning Bible Study

Begin your personal Bible study time with this prayer:

"Open my eyes that I may see wonderful things in Your law."
Psalms 119:18

Choose a verse from each study to place in your memory bank.
You will never be poor if you do.

Template #1

Date:_____

What passage I read today:_____

What I underlined:_____

Why it impressed me:_____

What am I going to do about it:_____

Template #2

Scripture passage:_____

I read to verse_____until God spoke to me.

This is what He is saying to me:_____

I prayed the following:_____

Template #3

Scripture passage:_____
What did it say?
What did it mean?
What did it mean to me?
Who did I share it with?

Template #4

Scripture passage:_____
List who, what, where information
Is there a description of God, Jesus Christ or the Holy Spirit?
Is there a sin to confess?
Is there an example to follow?
Is there a command to obey?
Is there a promise to claim?

"Eyes on God"
Tips on Prayer

Keep a list of God's answers to increase your faith in the dailies of life. We forget so easily what we prayed and how God answered! He loves answering, and He loves being thanked. Plus, He knows we grow stronger, the more we pray and acknowledge His work and thank Him.

There's nothing more encouraging than reading a list of how God has answered prayers in the past. You might want to frame it!

Some helpful tips:

- Pray Scripture back to God.
- Confess as soon as God convicts (He knows, anyway) On a regular basis, use David's words in Psalm 51, followed by Psalm 32 to repent and then enter into restoration.
- List God's attributes in your mind as you pray to remind you He's in charge and in love with you. Use Psalm 103 to help you in this exercise.
- Write out your prayers.
- Pray out loud when no one is around.
- Change your position in prayer.
- Look for answers.
- Use a journal to keep a record of answered prayers.
- Spend a whole day only thanking and praising God
- Use a spiral index card notebook on a key ring to keep track of family and friends' long-term prayer requests. Group by days of the week so that people we love the most and best get regular intercession time. Use a holiday family gathering to ask for current prayer requests in one-on-one dialogues.

What keeps us from praying:

- We try to solve our own problems first
- We forget how big God is
- We forgot how dependent we are
- We forget what He's done for us in the past
- We forget how much He loves us
- We forget how much He wants us to talk to Him
- We get lazy, complacent, and self-focused (ouch!)

"With God, no problem is too big and no detail is too small."
—Woodrow Kroll

"We have to pray with our eyes on God, not on our difficulties."
—Oswald Chambers

Appendix

Attributes of a Mentor and a Mentee

Mentors—this is who we need you to be:

- **Be a cheerleader**—we all need someone in our corner and on our balcony encouraging us in our journey towards becoming who God intends

- **Be a confidant**—we all need someone we can tell our concerns and burdens to with confidence

- **Be a mirror**—we all need someone who helps us be honest with ourselves

- **Be transparent**—we all need someone who has been there (and done that) and can share how God was faithful to her

- **Be an arrow**—we all need someone to direct us to the truth of God and His word in love

- **Be a listener**—we all need someone to ask us the hard questions and listen to our heart behind our words

- **Be growing**—we all need someone who is living a current life in the trenches of faith

Mentees—this is who we need you to be:

- **Be excited**—God's given you someone who's coming alongside to be your encourager

- **Be committed**—help your mentor develop your program and stick with it

- **Be hungry**—go after all that God wants you to taste and see

- **Be believing**—that God will do a good work in you as you work together

- **Be encouraged**—you won't grow up overnight, rejoice in the baby steps

- **Be grateful**—God's brought you to a friend who will help make you more like Jesus

- **Be prayerful**—God chooses to empower our growth and strengthen our relationship through consistent communication

Biblical Pattern of Growth

Spiritual growth is enhanced through prayer, Scripture memorization, church attendance, and accountability.

To encourage you along the way, here's a list of Bible passages on growth. Pick one to put to memory. These samples are from New International Version—choose a different translation if you prefer, but do choose one:

Growth is modeled by Paul.

"I don't mean to say that I have already achieved these things or that I have already reached perfection. But I press on to possess that perfection for which Christ Jesus first possessed me. No, dear brothers and sisters, I have not achieved it,[d] but I focus on this one thing: Forgetting the past and looking forward to what lies ahead, I press on to reach the end of the race and receive the heavenly prize for which God, through Christ Jesus, is calling us."

Philippians 3:12-14

Growth involves a balance of knowledge and relationship.

"...but speaking the truth in love, we are to grow up in all aspects into Him who is the head, even Christ..."

Ephesians 4:15

Growth is something we trust God for.

"In all my prayers for all of you, I always pray with joy 5 because of your partnership in the gospel from the first day until now, 6 being confident of this, that he who began a good work in you will carry it on to completion until the day of Christ Jesus."

Philippians 1:4-6

Growth takes continuous prayer.

"For this reason, since the day we heard about you, we have not stopped praying for you. We continually ask God to fill you with the knowledge of his will through all the wisdom and understanding that the Spirit gives, so that you may live a life worthy of the Lord and please him in every way: bearing fruit in every good work, growing in the knowledge of God.."

Colossians 1:9,10

Growth involves our not giving up.

"Therefore leaving the elementary teaching about the Christ, let us press on to maturity, not laying again a foundation of repentance from dead works and of faith toward God.."

Hebrews 6:1

Growth comes in layers as we lay ourselves before God in surrender.

"Now for this very reason also, applying all diligence, in your faith supply moral excellence, and in your moral excellence, knowledge, and in your knowledge, self-control, and in your self-control, perseverance, and in your perseverance, godliness…"

II Peter 1:5,6

Growth is our response to God's grace and for His glory.

"Therefore, dear friends, since you have been forewarned, be on your guard so that you may not be carried away by the error of the lawless and fall from your secure position. But grow in the grace and knowledge of our Lord and Savior Jesus Christ. To him be glory both now and forever! Amen."

II Peter 3:17,18

Growth is enhanced by involvement with others.

"And let us consider how we may spur one another on toward love and good deeds, [25] not giving up meeting together, as some are in the habit of doing, but encouraging one another—and all the more as you see the Day approaching."

Hebrews 10:24, 25

Growth results from our keeping our eyes on Christ.

And we all, who with unveiled faces contemplate the Lord's glory, are being transformed into his image with ever-increasing glory, which comes from the Lord, who is the Spirit.

II Corinthians 3:18

Add your own favorite verse on growing for Jesus' sake and for yours:

Advantages of a Personal Growth Plan

"It is what God makes you in the meantime that is the value of a big goal."
—Hyatt Moore

When your mentee designs her own plan, she is more vested in its progression.

An intentional plan:

- accelerates the growth process

- helps us focus on areas about which God is speaking to us

- encourages us to keep growing as we chart our progress

- keeps our focus clear: "What is it that God wants from me in this area?"

- facilitates healing; in the midst of a crisis or painful situation, our goals help us get up in the morning and place one foot in front of the other

- makes progress measurable for both the mentor and the mentee

- enables mutual accountability

- gives purpose and focus to your actions

"If you don't make goals, others will make them for you. Fifteen minutes a day will get you closer to your goals."
—Elizabeth George

All Church Women's Mentoring Event

Our church puts on an all-church women's mentoring event two or three times a year. It's a great way to cross-pollinate age groups, build community and allow new mentors to try out sharing their expertise on a one-time basis. And it's a whole lot of fun with minimum effort.

How we do it:

Invite a group of women to lead a table on a topic in which they feel comfortable sharing. Let them know you aren't looking for experts or a three-point sermon; just an opportunity to come alongside other women and share their experience. Give them simple guidelines on how to spark a discussion with their table ladies and lead them to truth in Scripture.

Charge $5.00 at the door to cover costs of treats, decorations and maybe an outside speaker.

Giveaways are a blast. When the ladies arrive they receive a quarter sheet on which they provide their contact information (for follow–up down the road) and after filling it out, they place it in a basket in front of a donated door prize. Halfway through the evening, names are drawn and people are happy. Everyone loves a present!

Also at the door, each receives a list of the table topics and who's leading and they can meander around the room and figure how where they want to "land" for the evening. They can choose to go to two different tables: Session I and II.

Allow time for beverages and snacks at the beginning and perhaps a bigger treat at the halfway point – between Session I and Session II. If there is a main speaker, make it no more than 20 minutes so that the emphasis is on spending time around the tables.

Plan for guests to sit in on two different mentoring topic tables. Sort of like "speed dating"! Women move one table to the next – not to get a date – but to get some practical and spiritual knowledge to help all grow up in Christ. It's a blast and I always make at least one new friend! I provide a hand out, but others lead with a few good questions and facilitate an informal discussion. It's important to allow time for questions and discussion.

Our last Mentor Night was a "Mad Hatter" theme and we had tea and scones and sliders.

Table Topics:

Mentoring, 101
Fresh ways to delve deeper into Scripture
How to get involved in your community
Intentional Grandparenting
Guarding against negative self-talk
Raising young kids
Organizing your life
Learning the art of surrender
Managing a busy household
Discovering your God given strengths
Dealing with depression & anxiety
Beyond bedtime prayers:
    How to go deeper in your time with God

Other evenings, topics included:

How to Memorize Scripture (and Keep it Memorized)
Hospitality
Personal Bible Study
Neighborhood Outreach
How to Memorize Scripture
Parenting Teens
Nurturing Your Marriage
Bible Journaling
Balancing Your Best Self

A great bonus is that some new mentoring relationships have begun as a result of this fun evening out. Older women meeting with younger, coming alongside and giving to one another what God's given them.

Any questions? Contact Angela Anderson at Grace Central Coast, San Luis Obispo, CA
angela@gracecentralcoast.org

What Should We Study?

The Navigators leader from the local university approached our Women's Ministry Director and asked for some formal mentoring to be offered to young college women. Some had just become believers and needed immediate guidance from an older Christian woman. From that need, we set up a six-week program on six different topics. We met in a home one night a week and began teaching what we knew.

Topics included:

Budgeting
Meal Planning
Quiet times
Hospitality

When you ask your mentee: "What would you like to get out of our time together?" you will get an idea of where to begin. One summer I asked my mentor: "How can I learn to love Jesus more?" She found a study book and we did it together through the next two months.

From the mentees:
"What did you learn from your mentor?"

I learned how to be a Christian woman, how to study the Bible, how to love my kids, and family, and husband, and others.

–Brittany

I learned how to keep the faith no matter what. God is sovereign through our suffering and has a plan. My mentor has been a walking, talking, praying, faith filled example of this to me.

–Janelle

I learned a lot about myself. I l learned that God is faithful. I learned that mentoring makes a difference. I learned that mentoring relationships many times are seasons of life but they are so deep that they last a lifetime and have a unique impact that you don't get in other surface relationships and even in small groups. To know you have one person in your corner cheering you on and supporting you in such an intense way makes you think you can do anything.

Even when you have a great family dynamic and a great husband having a mentor is a powerful thing.

–Melody H.

I learned how to view current circumstances with a better perspective. So helpful to have hope when hard times are being encountered. Parenting perspective from empty nesters was huge for helping us get through trying high school years with our kids.

–Gretchen

I learned so many insights. So much knowledge. I developed a love for Scripture memorization. I watched how they lived life and saw them modeling what that looks like.

–Laurie

I learned to love the Word and read it, early on. My first mentor led me as a 13 year old new believer to read John and I really learned who Jesus is. Later, to value the time invested in Christian books and doing one with a mentor. Learned the value of a real friendship between two sisters in Christ and the love and care shared.

–Emily

I loved being encouraged. Being provided with guidance. Having someone's guidance to balance with God's Word and my own experience. Being held accountable by someone other than my mom.

–Jaime

So the topic matters: teaching another to trust and know God better and deeper. And the relationship between mentor and mentee matters just as much–be transparent, be biblical, be prayerful, be committed.

For the Mentor/Mentee Library

Devotional Reading:

Face to Face   Kenneth Boa

My Utmost for His Highest   Oswald Chambers

Daily Light   Anne Graham Lotz

Daily with the King   Glyn Evans

Jesus Calling   Sarah Evans

The Seeking Heart   Fenelon

Life of the Beloved   Henri Nouwen

Grace Notes   Philip Yancey

The Pursuit of God   A.W. Tozer

Topical and Bible Studies:

Women Encouraging Women   Lucibel Van Atta

Disciplines of a Beautiful Woman   Anne Ortlund

Jesus Cares for Women   Helene Ashker

Becoming a Woman of Excellence   Cynthia Heald

Women of the Word   Jen Wilkin

Being a Mary in a Martha World   Joanna Weaver

Come Walk with Me   Carole Mayhall

Calm My Anxious Heart   Linda Dillow

What Love Is   Kelly Minter

Come to My Table: God's Hospitality and Yours   Sue Moore Donaldson

Hospitality 101: Lessons from the Ultimate Host   Sue Moore Donaldson

About Sue

Sue Moore Donaldson and her husband, Mark, live in San Luis Obispo, California. They have raised three semi-adult daughters who keep them at the bank and on their knees. Sue loves connecting women to one another, to God and to His Word, and has been speaking for the last twenty years or so with long pauses for babies, diapers and soccer pasta parties. Sue's practical books on hospitality continue to inspire men and women to open their homes and set another place for the sake of the Gospel and to come alongside. *Come to My Table: God's Hospitality and Yours* and *Hospitality 101: Lessons from the Ultimate Host– A 12-Week Bible Study.*

Connect with Sue

Sue's Website
welcomeheart.com

Follow on Facebook
You're invited to join our Welcome Heart, Welcome Home Facebook group. Please pull up your chair to Sue's Table, and send your Table story to Every Table Tells a Story Facebook group.

Follow on Instagram
#everytabletellsastory and #suemooredonaldson

Follow on Twitter
@welcomeheart

Email Sue your favorite recipe and share your stories that God has used and told at your table.
sue@welcomeheart.com

TABLE MENTORING

Made in the USA
Monee, IL
14 June 2021